# PARENTING ISN'T
# EASY BUT WORTH IT

# PARENTING ISN'T EASY BUT WORTH IT

DR. SHIRLEY DURHAM

ARPress
ILLUMINATING IDEAS.
EMPOWERING VOICES

**ARPress**
45 Dan Road Suite 5
Canton MA 02021
Hotline:        1(888) 821-0229
Fax:            1(508) 545-7580

Ordering Information:

Quantity sales. Special discounts are available on quantity purchases by corporations, associations, and others. For details, contact the publisher at the address above.

Printed in the United States of America.

ISBN-13:        Paperback       979-8-89330-689-7
                eBook           979-8-89330-688-0

Library of Congress Control Number: 2024902530

# TABLE OF CONTENTS

# AKNOWLEDGEMENT

To my amazing, husband of thirty years,

Dr. Harold G. Durham

My husband was pursuing me, for marriage.

One of my concerns was,

Could I handle four children? He said to me.

God said you can!

I am grateful that thirty years later.

We have five children, Erva,  Porshua, Robert,

Tiffany, and Donelle.

They are all college graduates and self-sustaining.

Four incredible grandchildren,

who are a gift from God.

To God Be the Glory!

# INTRODUCTION

This book came about after working in childcare for 35 years. Seeing parents bring their children into the center and leave them with us for eight to ten hours. My concern was how parent allow themselves to be ok with leaving their children with total strangers.

I settle to work in childcare to keep my children with me, while being employed. To keep from dealing with emotional separation and regret. My son Erva who is thirty-eight and a daughter Porshua, who is twenty-nine. I have three in heritage children, Robert who is forty, Tiffany is thirty-nine, and Donelle is thirty-seven.

My rationale for writing this book particularly for parents who are in a despair moment asking themselves why did I have children?

Children are a Blessing in disguise. After they are born you realize what a precious human being created by God.

How do you love this God given gift that has dirty diapers, spit up on you, keep you up late in the midnight hours, has early stages of manipulation. Breaks sentimental values, shows no appreciation for your kindness. They have some entitlement to what you have worked years to accomplish.

At the end of the day, we will love our children forever and as long as they are living our babies they will be.

It is my desire to share with you experiences of being a mother and Child Development Educator for over 35 years.

# POEM- UNKNOWN

Listen to your children
Take A Moment To Listen Today
To What Your Children
What They Are Trying To Say
Listen Today Whatever You Do
Or They Want Be There
To Listen To You
Listen To Their Problems
Listen To Their Needs
Praise Their Smallest Triumph
Praise Their Smallest Deeds
Tolerate Their Chatter
Amplify Their Laughter
Find Out What's The Matter
Find Out What They're After
Tell Them That You Love Them
Every Single Night
And Though You Scold Them
Be Sure You Hold Them Tight
And Tell Them
Everything's All Right
And Tomorrow is Looking Bright
Take A Moment  To Listen Today
To Hear What They Are Trying To Say
Listen Today Whatever You Do
And They Will Come Back To You

# Ages and Stages

## 0-12 Months

When the new baby comes home it is a new learning experience. To be a Mother or a Father is the greatest title you will receive without having to earn it. There is nothing like being a parent. Knowing, what to do, and what not to do, can be overwhelming. Learning to manage your life after having a child requires research and asking questions, from experienced experts, whose children are making great progress.

At this age the brain is still developing. The baby's brain grows rapidly until the age of three. Nutritious food, playtime, talking, and singing to your baby, laughing, cuddling, will help your baby's brain develop. You don't need a cookbook to have nutritious food for babies. During the first six months it is giving your child a nutritious liquid diet. Don't allow yourself to be discouraged if you can't produce breast milk. There are other ways and means to provide nutritious feeding for your baby. As you talk with your child Pediatrician you should come to an agreement to know what is best for your baby.

When your baby is six months old it is time to introduce your baby to food that is easy to chew. Always keep in mind the development of your baby's brain. Being selective of the type of food that is healthy, like berries, beans, vegetables, and meat in puree, or mashed, making sure cooked food is blended. You can buy pre- purée baby foods. When your baby has teeth introduce them to solid food with texture, like soft carrots.

In early childhood the brain is eager to form a new connection. Help your baby build brain connections by providing a safe environment and bonding with your baby, forming a strong attachment by responding to the needs of your baby.

Luke 2:6-7

## 13 TO 17 MONTHS

At this stage you are learning to communicate with your baby, their babbling is starting to sound more like talking. He may say "mama" and really is sincere when he says it. Parents are excited to hear their baby say mama or dada. It's exciting to hear your baby as they begin to name things. At this stage babies love to play games. Show your baby things that can make noises. Take a blanket and cover the things that make noise. See if your baby can identify with things that are noisy.

When possible, take some quiet time with your baby. Listen to soft music, with your baby. Hold your baby close to you and tell them that you love them. Talk to your baby about what they are doing. Let your baby see your face and watch your lips as words come out of your mouth. Talk calmly and have a conversation.

Show your baby how to clap and sing along while having rhythm. Dance with your baby. Your baby will enjoy moving to the beat. As you play music watch as your baby responds to different kinds of music.

Let your baby hear the voice of daddy or grandparents on the phone and watch as the smile with excitement, the more they hear them on the phone this will help with recognition and identify.

As you prepare meals and do the duties of the day for the family set your baby in an area where they can see you. Encourage your precious one to use two or more words together, to make small conversation like "Help Me" or "More Please. These words will begin to become more words, and lots of communication.

Read to your baby every day. Make it a special time; embrace your baby as you read to her. Notice how they will have favorite books they would like you to read to them. Ask question about what they see in the book and ask them to point it out. Like Where is the Pig.

Your baby can be a big Helper. Asked him to pick up the toys and put them on the shelf. Sing as you help put the toy where they belong, Sing, "Picking up the Circle." Put' um in the basket."

Take your baby for a walk outside. Name the things you see on the outside and say the colors of the things you are seeing. Let your baby feel nature the dirt, water, and grass. Point out the birds, bees and butterflies.

Give your child hope and confidence. Give baby a ball and let them throw it to you. Do it over and over. Talk about how far he can throw it.

Make things at home. Use the things you have at home to teach your child. With your empty container talk about sizes and colors. Let your child stack things on top of each other, from smallest to largest.

These small things that you do with your baby are the most precious moments that will last for a lifetime.

## 19 to 24 Months

When I worked in childcare, this was my favorite age. I enjoyed seeing the independency of toddlers having determination and persistency. Their favorite word is no, and their favorite phrase is I can do it.

My grandson Ian, broke his arm at the age of two. When he came to visit us with his cast on his arm, he would come to the table pull out the chair, lay his tummy on the seat and find a way to straighten his body and sit on the chair he did not want to sit in the highchair, and he would say I can do it.

At this age, you can expect new complex emotions, pre-toddlers likes pretending play, independence, walking, saying a lot of new words, and climbing on furniture. Having activities for toddlers development include talking and listening, reading, working on everyday skills, and playing outside with others. One of their favorite games is hiding and seeking. Toddlers enjoys taking their shoes off. When my son Erva, was 18 months he enjoyed taking off his one shoe and throwing it across the room and then he would run to find it. Toddlers loves to build with blocks and watch them fall down. Toddlers can be still while changing the diapers. Toddlers enjoy being chased by others. Toddlers begin to recognize facial expressions. You can ask them to name parts of their body. Ask toddlers to tell you what they like and don't like. Toddlers can help around the house. They can pick up the toy and put them on the shelves. Toddlers likes to hold your hand and walk around the room. Toddles become attached to certain things that become a favorite to them. Parent has to safe proof their home for this age making sure you have safe proof electrical outlet. Male toddle likes to jump off tables and chairs. Toddlers like different textures. They are fascinated with new things.

You can begin to potty train your child. This is the age where children are very observance. They will watch what you are doing and begin to imitate older children and adults. Toddlers enjoy seeing pictures of themselves and people they know. For instance, like mommy and daddy, grandparents, and their sibling.

Keep in mind that all children's development is not the same. If you are concerned about your child's development, talk with your medical child's medical provider.

A child needs love, understanding, protection and provision. Your time with your child in a happy and healthy environment will help your child with courage and confidence, to have a strong foundation.

# PRESCHOOL AGE

At this age children are more independent and learn to explore, they will ask questions, about things that surround them; and enjoy being with other children outside their family. Preschool interaction with families and other adults will shape their personalities, and their own way of thinking and movement.

Anxiety, worries and fear are part of preschool development. They can display mix emotions, energy, shyness, fighting, lying , and habits. Most parents find it difficult to understand the behavior of a preschooler. The parent is used to getting out the clothing they want their child to wear and the child tells them "I don't want to wear that." The parents may process this to be a struggle, when it can be an opportunity to observe the child's creativity, their likes and dislikes.

When Preschooler is in a learning environment with other children, they show great quality in social and emotional skills. Preschoolers likes to be around people and they like people to notice them. They may ask you if you like their hair and their shoes. If you start complimenting other preschoolers around them, they will ask you "do you like their clothing." This age is a very competitive age, and their curiosity causes them to experiment new things.

Developing friends at this age is helping the preschooler to share with others. Most of the things that are given to them they take ownership, and refuse to allow others to be engaged with what belongs to them.

This age is the groundwork for the future. Children learn as they are playing, singing, and socializing, with their age group. They will learn a lot about themselves, and how to interact appropriately with others.

When the child is being picked up from the childcare center, often times the parent would ask their child, "what you learned today," the child would say, "I just played." This can be frustrating to a parent, when they are paying or having someone to spend most of the day with their precious little ones.

When children have a holistic and well-rounded educational environment they will learn through play. If parents are educated and empowered about their child's development, they can be involved and connected with their child's progress.

## OFF TO KINDERGARTEN

My goodness, where did the time go? So much has transpired in these five years. You began to reflect on the day you brought your child home from the hospital. When your child walks into the classroom with his crest jeans, dressed shirt and shiny forehead, and he let your hand go as if he had found a whole new adventure. I knew he was going to be alright. Sending our son Erva, to a predominantly all white school named Western Hill Elementary, in White Settlement, Texas. It was encouraging to know that my child had the confidence, and boldness that he was in a safe place.

I believe this is the first stage of letting go, however you really do not let go, your psychological conditions your mind to release and move forward from unhealthy emotions. As parents, our children are important to us, so we love them; and realize it is detrimental to our well-being if we don't let go and allow them to grow.

As we converse about our belief of letting go, we are not referring to physically grasping with our hands. In counseling we tell our clients, letting go is more about mentally releasing our attachment to something. Preferably struggling to keep someone in our lives or insisting on a particular out outcome, we relinquish that need or craving and instead accept what is or what must transpire. We must accept what God allows. Be willing to experience, thoughts and emotions as a vital component of what it means to let go.

As a person, we have a tendency to hold onto things; even those that we know are harmful to us. One reliable statement is that the more we understand ourselves, the more we appreciate our own identity.

It can be intimidating when you are uncertain about the outcome of destiny. Consequently, we might find ourselves stuck, clinging to both positive and negative aspects of our lives, apprehensive about letting go.

Just a little story about our lovely daughter Porshua, I was so attached to her, that I did not want her to go to Public School. So, I started a Private School at our childcare facility, and hired a teacher to teach six children. She started Public school in the second grade. I found it so hard to send her to a place where I was not going to be there. At this point, is when I realize it was more about me than what is best for my child.

I had to learn how to be optimistic, when letting go. I began to focus on the positive sense of the future and maintain an optimist outlook. If we expect to fail, we are more likely to do so.

"Children are a gift from the Lord; they are a reward from Him." Psalm 127:3NLT. Start at a young age to let go of your children to age and maturity secure experiences.

## THE EXCEPTION IN ELEMENTARY

During the school-age years, you'll see a change in your child. He or she will move from playing alone to having multiple friends and social groups. Friendships become more important. But your child is still fond of you as a parent, and likes being part of a family. Children progress at different rates. They have different interests, abilities, and personalities. But there are some common milestones many children reach from ages 6 to 12.

As your child grows, you'll notice him or her developing new and exciting abilities.

## A CHILD AGE 6 TO 7:

- Enjoys many activities and stays busy.

- Likes to paint and draw.

- Practices skills in order to become better.

- Jumps rope.

- Rides a bike.

## A CHILD AGE 8 TO 9:

- Is more graceful with movements and abilities.

- Jumps, skips, and chases.

- Dresses and grooms self completely.

- Can use tools, such as a hammer or screwdriver.

- Likes to sew and paint.

## A child age 10 to 12:

- Writes stories.

- Likes to write letters.

- Reads well.

- Enjoys using the telephone.

### WHAT DOES MY CHILD UNDERSTAND?

An important part of growing up is learning to interact and socialize with others. During the school-age years, you'll see a change in your child. He or she will move from playing alone to having multiple friends and social groups. Friendships become more important. But your child is still fond of you as a parent, and likes being part of a family. Below are some of the common traits that your child may show at these ages.

As children enter into school age, their skills and understanding of concepts continue to grow.

## A CHILD AGE 6 TO 7:

- Understands the concept of numbers.

- Knows daytime and nighttime.

- Knows right and left hands.

- Can copy complex shapes, such as a diamond.

- Can tell time.

- Understands commands that have 3 separate instructions.

- Can explain objects and their use.

- Can repeat 3 numbers backward.

- Can read age-appropriate books.

- A child age 8 to 9:

- Can count backward.

- Knows the date.

- Reads more and enjoys reading.

- Understands fractions.

- Understands the concept of space.

- Draws and paints.

- Can name the months and days of the week in order.

- Enjoys collecting objects.

# HOW WILL MY CHILD INTERACT WITH OTHERS?

An important part of growing up is learning to interact and socialize with others. During the school-age years, you'll see a change in your child. He or she will move from playing alone to having multiple friends and social groups. Friendships become more important. But your child is still fond of you as parents, and likes being part of a family. Below are some of the common traits that your child may show at these ages.

### A child age 6 to 7:

- Cooperates and shares.

- Can be jealous of others and siblings.

- Likes to copy adults.

- Likes to play alone, but friends are becoming important.

- Plays with friends of the same gender.

- May sometimes have temper tantrums.

- Is modest about his or her body.

- Likes to play board games.

**A child age 8 to 9:**

- Likes competition and games.

- Starts to mix friends and play with children of the opposite gender.

- Is modest about his or her body.

- Enjoys clubs and groups, such as Boy Scouts or Girl Scouts.

- Is becoming interested in boy-girl relationships but doesn't admit it.

**A child age 10 to 12:**

- Finds friends are very important and may have a best friend.

- Has increased interest in the opposite gender.

- Likes and respects parents.

- Enjoys talking to others.

## HOW CAN I ENCOURAGE MY CHILD'S SOCIAL ABILITIES?

You can help boost your school-aged child's social abilities by:

- Setting limits, guidelines, and expectations and enforcing them with appropriate penalties.

- Modeling good behavior.

- Complimenting your child for being cooperative and for personal achievements.

- Helping your child choose activities that are suitable for his or her abilities.

- Encouraging your child to talk with you and be open with his or her feelings.

- Encouraging your child to read, and reading with your child.

- Encouraging your child to get involved with hobbies and other activities.

- Promoting physical activity.

- Encouraging self-discipline and expecting your child to follow rules that are set.

- Teaching your child to respect and listen to authority figures.

- Encouraging your child to talk about peer pressure and setting guidelines to deal with peer pressure.

- Spending uninterrupted time together and giving full attention to your child.

- Limiting screen time (TV, video, and computer).

## AGES 13 TO 17

Human development is a lifelong process of physical, behavioral, cognitive, and emotional growth and change. In the early stages of life— from babyhood to childhood, childhood to adolescence, and adolescence to adulthood—enormous changes take place. Throughout the process, each person develops attitudes and values that guide choices, relationships, and understanding. Sexuality is also a lifelong process. Infants, children, teens, and adults are sexual beings. Just as it is important to enhance a child's physical, emotional, and cognitive growth, so it is important to lay foundations for a child's sexual growth. Adults have a responsibility to help children understand and accept their evolving sexuality. Each stage of development encompasses specific markers. The following developmental guidelines apply to most children in this age group. However, each child is an individual and may reach these stages of development earlier or later than other children the same age. When concerns arise about a specific child's development, parents or other caregivers should consult a doctor or other child development professional. Note: When we use the words "males" and "females" and "boys" and "girls," we are referring to those who are assigned male or female at birth and have corresponding body parts, independent of gender identity.

## PHYSICAL DEVELOPMENT

Most teens ages 13 to 17 will:

- Reach nearly their adult height, especially females (males continue to grow taller into their early twenties.)

## PHYSICAL DEVELOPMENT

Most teens ages 13 to 17 will:

- Reach nearly their adult height, especially females (males continue to grow taller into their early twenties.)

- Complete puberty and the physical transition from childhood to adulthood.

## COGNITIVE DEVELOPMENT

Most teens ages 13 to 17 will:

- Attain cognitive maturity—the ability to make decisions based on knowledge of options and their consequences.

- Continue to be influenced by peers (The power of peer pressure lessens after early adolescence.)

- Build skills to become self-sufficient.

- Respond to media messages but develop increasing ability to analyze those messages.

- Develop increasingly mature relationships with friends and family.

- Seek increased power over their own lives.

- Learn to drive, increasing their independence.

## EMOTIONAL DEVELOPMENT

Most teens ages 13 to 17 will:

- Have the capacity to develop long-lasting, mutual, and healthy relationships, if they have the foundations for this development—trust, positive past experiences, and an understanding of love.

- Understand their own feelings and have the ability to analyze why they feel a certain way.

- Begin to place less value on appearance and more on personality.

## SEXUAL DEVELOPMENT

Most teens ages 13 to 17 will:

- Understand that they are sexual and understand the options and consequences of sexual expression.

- Choose to express their sexuality in ways that may or may not include shared sexual behaviors.

- Recognize the components of healthy and unhealthy relationships.

- Have a clear understanding of pregnancy and of HIV and other sexually transmitted infections.

- Recognize the impact various media have on cultural views about sex.

- Have the capacity to learn about intimate, loving, long-term relationships.

- Have an understanding of their own sexual orientation (This is different than sexual behavior)

## WHAT FAMILIES NEED TO DO TO RAISE SEXUALLY HEALTHY TEENS

To help teens ages 13 to 17 develop as sexually healthy youth, families should:

- Clearly articulate your family and religious values regarding sexual intercourse. Express that, although sex is pleasurable, young people should wait to initiate sex until they are in a mature, loving, and responsible relationship.

- Express that we all have a variety of options for experiencing intimacy and expressing love.

- Discuss together the factors, including age, mutual consent, protection, contraceptive use, love, intimacy, etc., that you and your teen believe should be a part of decisions about sexual intercourse.

- Reinforce teens' ability to make decisions while providing information on which they can base those decisions.

- Discuss contraceptive options and talk about the importance of condom use.

- Discuss teens' options, should unprotected intercourse occur — including emergency contraception and STI testing and treatment. Discuss teens' options, should pregnancy occur, including abortion, parenting, and adoption.

- Discuss exploitive behavior and why it is unhealthy and (in some cases) illegal.

Help youth identify various physical and verbal responses to avoid/ get away from sexual situations that make them feel uncomfortable.

## 10 TIPS ON INITIATING CONVERSATIONS ABOUT GROWTH

Initiating conversations about growth, development, and sexuality may be difficult for some parents because they did not grow up in an environment where the subject was discussed. Some parents may be afraid they do not know the right answers or feel confused about the proper amount of information to offer. To help, consider these 10 tips:

1. First, encourage communication by reassuring your children that they can talk with you about anything.

2. Take advantage of teachable moments. A friend's pregnancy, news article, or a TV show can help start a conversation.

3. Listen more than you talk. Think about what you're being asked. Confirm with your child that what you heard is in fact what they meant to ask.

4. Don't jump to conclusions. The fact that a teen asks about sex does not mean they are having or thinking about having sex.

5. Answer questions simply and directly. Give factual, honest, short, and simple answers.

6. Respect your child's views. Share your thoughts and values and help your child express theirs.

7. Reassure young people that they are normal— as are their questions and thoughts.

8. Teach your children ways to make good decisions about sex and coach them on how to get out of risky situations.

9. Admit when you don't know the answer to a question. Suggest the two of you find the answer together online or in the library.

10. Discuss that at times your teen may feel more comfortable talking with someone other than you. Together, think of other trusted adults with whom they can talk.

# ADULT AGE CHILDREN

In your eyes, your child will always be "your child," no matter what their age, but in the eyes of the law, that "child" is legally an adult on their 18th birthday.

When our young child reaches the age eighteen, in the state of Texas, this is the age where they are considered to be an adult.

As a parent there are some documents, such as ID's, birth certificate, social security card, that you want to be available and in a safe place. If you don't have certain documents in place, this can cause hardship for you and your son or daughter. You will not be able to make legal decisions on their behalf and lose the ability to access any of their health, education, or financial or financial records.

During college enrollment the administrator had our children sign a document that would allow us to get information concerning them. Isn't it amazing you have taken care of them all these years and now you have to have permission to get information about them?

Furthermore, in the unanticipated situation where your child is incapable of making decisions on their own, you will be barred from making them on their behalf. This can present a unique set of challenges if your child is away at college. Planning for these and other issues that may arise is vital to avoiding the various pitfalls that you and your children may face.

## WHAT DOCUMENTS SHOULD YOU CONSIDER HAVING IN PLACE ON YOUR CHILD'S 18TH BIRTHDAY?

**Health care power of attorney.** Often referred to as a "health care proxy," this document is essential because it gives you the authority to make health care decisions on behalf of your child. Health care proxies don't normally kick in unless your child is determined to be physically or mentally incapable of making decisions on their own. It's a scenario you never want to have to consider as a parent, but it's a document you will be thankful to have in place if you ever need it.

**HIPAA authorization.** The Health Insurance Portability and Accountability Act, otherwise known as HIPAA, is a privacy law that prevents health care providers from disclosing your child's current medical condition or medical records to unauthorized persons. If you want to maintain access to that information, a HIPAA authorization document must be on file. Additionally, if your child feels uncomfortable allowing unrestricted access to their sensitive information, he or she can limit its breadth according to their comfort level.

**Financial power of attorney.** Similar to the health care proxy, the financial power of attorney allows you to make financial decisions and access financial records on your child's behalf. The list of benefits is long as to why it is a good idea to have this in place, but a practical reason is simply that if they are getting ready to head off to college, details like tax deadlines, contractual obligations, and other time-sensitive financial decisions can be easily overlooked amongst their busy schedules. By exercising the authority granted in a Power of Attorney, you may be able to maintain access to these matters, and you and your child may be able to avoid some headaches or costly mistakes that could result if these details were overlooked.

**FERPA authorization.** FERPA stands for the Family Educational Rights and Privacy Act, which requires that students over age 18 give written consent before any educational records can be released to another person. "Educational records" is broadly defined under FERPA to mean those records that are: (1) directly related to the student, and (2) maintained by an educational agency or institution acting for the agency or institution. Of course, this include transcripts, disciplinary actions, scholarship information, and tuition information, but what is less apparent is that records maintained by the college campus's health clinic are also considered an "educational record" and therefore not covered under HIPAA. For example, if your child visits his or her university's health services center for treatment, you would not have access to his or her medical records merely by presenting a signed HIPAA form. By way of contrast, however, if your child is sent to the local hospital for treatment, then the HIPAA form would permit you to access his or her medical information.

**Simple will.** If your adult child dies owning assets, his or her estate is subject to the probate laws of their state of domicile. If the child does not have a will or will substitute, any individually owned assets will pass according to the intestate laws of the state. Generally, the assets of an unmarried child with no descendants will pass to his or her parents, if they are living. If the parents are not living, the assets will go to their siblings. Although the appropriateness of a will or will substitute varies based on the complexity of the child's estate, you should consider discussing this with your adult child.

## UNIFORM GIFTS TO MINORS ACT (UGMA) AND UNIFORM TRANSFERS TO MINORS ACT (UTMA) ACCOUNTS

My husband and I set up bank accounts for our children when they were 13 years old. When they started working as a teen, they were aware it was a requirement for them to put 10% to the church and 10% to saving. When our sons, and daughters, left home for college, they were surprised about the amount of money they had saved.

UGMA and UTMA accounts are custodial accounts set up for minors that can hold cash, investments, and, in some cases, collectables. These accounts are controlled by a custodian, usually the parent. Depending on state law, when the child attains age 18[1] or 21[2], he or she assumes control of the account.

### BEYOND THE LEGAL REQUIREMENTS

Dealing with the legal aspect, of course, is just part of this journey for you and your child. Turning 18 is an important milestone and an opportunity for you to engage in meaningful conversations about your hopes and wishes as well as getting an idea of your child's dreams.

Making sure you have the legal documents described above will give you access to important information, but, ideally, much of this information will come via speaking with your child. If your child will be away from home, discussing how much contact and what method will vary by child. It'll also be a time for your child to stretch their wings and build their own experiences. Some may discover that their initial choice, whether it be college or career, may not be right for them, or they may not be making the most of the experience. This is an opportunity for you to coach them on being accountable as well as finding their own path. Whether your child is nearing their 18th birthday or has already crossed that milestone, consider the steps outlined above to help you both be prepared for the exciting journey called life.

## MAKING PARENTING WORTH IT

Being a mother was one of the greatest desires, I had in life. I had the greatest experience in caring for my nieces and nephews at the age of ten. I would ride the bus to their house and cook for them. I would cut up a whole chicken, and fry it; and open a can of Pork and Beans, alone with opening a can of cream corn, also put store brought biscuits in the oven. While I was caring for these little people, I had no concept that this was preparing me to care for thousands of children in my lifetime.

Sometimes our expectations can be too much. As parents we want the best for our children. We are sometime not ready for them to make mistakes and have difficulties in life. I believe every parent, should be like the scripture says, about God. That He is a very present help in the time of trouble.

Parents have amnesia when their children start having challenges in life. If parents would rewind the tape and play it all the way through, they will realize some of the same situation that happen with their child, happened with them.

The King James Bible tells us Love covers multitudes of faults.

Create success for your child's life; assure them that failure is not the end. When they are raped up tied up and tangled up in confusion, comfort them and tell them they are going to be ok. Hug them often and allow them to experience the emotions of love and forgiveness.

The love of a family is the greatest gift you can allow your child to experience. Yet one single incident of abuse can cause great damage to your child. Emotional abuse is a pattern that causes damage over time. Physiological abuse causes damage to the child's self-worth and negative impact on the child emotional and social development.

Often time, parents can confuse discipline and abuse. Discipline is teaching rules and regulations, and you follow up on the consequences. Abuse is when you cross the limits to get your way, that you hurt a child and it leads sever physical, physiological and emotional damage.

## CULTURE INFLUENCES

Children will embrace different cultures by the environment they are raised. Such as culture can affect how children build values, language, belief systems, and understanding of themselves as a person and a member of society. Children receive these cultural influences in different ways, such as through their parents, their environment, and the media. Your cultural background can influence how you raise your children. You may have different parenting views to your family members, which can be stressful for your child. Find common ground and involve both cultures in your child's life, so they feel a sense of belonging and security. Teach your child about cultural differences outside of the home. This helps them respect others and themselves. Allow your child to interact with other cultures to avoid discrimination. So they will respect and understand culture differences to avoid, distrust and isolation, anger and frustration,

# HOW TO HANDLE CONFLICT IN THE HOME

It's common for parents and families to disagreements.

Disagreement in a home can be upsetting for your child, and conflicting rules can confuse them, if there is no clarity. Having limited choices can reduce conflicts, and reduce stress.

Disagreement in a multicultural home can be upsetting for your child, and conflicting rules can confuse them. They may also feel like they have to choose one culture over the other, which can be stressful.

## Spouses

If you and your spouse are from different cultures, you might have different ideas. Communication is the key to overcoming these issues.

Regardless of your cultural background, you should <u>talk to your spouse</u> about how you want your family to be. Try to find creative ways to raise your child in both cultures by:

- Speaking to your child in more than one language.
- telling them stories about your culture
- involving them in traditional celebrations

With your spouse, discuss which traditions and values you would like your family to follow. If you disagree, try to find the middle ground. This will help your child feel safe and secure with both of you. It will also help them learn about your culture and feel they belong.

## Family

If you experience conflict in your extended family, you and your spouse should work as a team. There is an old quote united we stand divided we fall. There is power in agreement.

Once you and your spouse agree on a parenting issue, discuss your decision you're your family units such as grandparents.

Family members often just want the best for you and your child. You can set boundaries to help you work together as a family to care for your child. Communicate with your partner and family by, standing up for yourself while still respecting their beliefs and feelings, speaking calmly and firmly, provide constructive criticism but not placing blame using calm, open body language, reminding them that you appreciate the good things they bring to the relationship, thanking them when they respect your boundaries.

# SHARING YOUR CHILDHOOD MEMORIES

Take your children to the place where you grow up and allow them to see the diversity of your upbringing. Have conversing dialog about how times have changed with the past and present age. I was born in a small town called Linden, Texas in Cass County

I was brought up in a very adorable family. My mother went to church on Sundays and Wednesdays she read the Bible us and often quoted scriptures; to us she graduated from high school. She stayed home and took care of the home, cooking, cleaning, washing clothes, hanging them on the clothesline to dry, making quilts, preserving food and helping us with our homework. She was a disciplinarian when she needed to be. She had the understanding of discipline and not abuse. She wanted us to know the difference between right and wrong. Our Sunday's dinner was roast beef with gravy, mash potatoes, red beans, cornbread and banana pudding. She passed away at the age of 84, Monday September 18, 2018.

Our father worked and provided for the family, he did not finish school, he showed us he loved us by spending time with us and telling us he loved us. He was 54 when he passed away, Monday February 18, 1980. Another beautiful thing I can remember is my dad would allow us to sit on the back of his brother station wagon and we would jump off and run and get be on. Holidays were the greatest, seeing our aunts, uncles and cousins, and eating delicious homemade food.

Another beautiful thing I can remember is my visiting our grandparents, who own lots of land, they live on a farm. We had fresh fruits and vegetable often. Their home is where we learned work ethics. Anytime we went to their house it was all work and no play. Perhaps the time I remember very fondly was when we had family reunions.

We have a large family. They would come from various places, smiles and hugs were contagious. Tables were outside with different kinds of food and drinks. The magical of my childhood was love.

Sharing your childhood memories will help you to connect with your children and allow them to connect with things you have in common.


## Honoring and Respect

In a world full of numerous of problems, the most dangerous to our children are drugs, abuse, poverty, gun violence, neglect, disease and others. How can we fix the problem? I say we because, we are in the world to make a difference to all of these ungodly sinful acts of mankind. If we would recognize the BIBLE the acronym basic instruction before leaving earth. The Bible is a guide to help us with this commodity in life.

When we lose honor and respect, we have lost a nation.

As Christians, God not only commands us to honor our parents, but also to be faithful in prayer. As we honor our parents by including them in our prayers, we obey both commands which is pleasing to God!

Parents should let their children hear them praying for their mom and dad. This will help you make connections that they can also pray for their parents. This will allow the children to understand we need God to help us with our problems. And we allow God to be the source to all our needs. Our children will know that we can take our request to God and he will answer us.

For those who struggle with their parents, prayer can also be a safe step of obedience. It doesn't require direct contact with anyone but God, meaning you don't have to see your parents or even be on speaking terms to pray for them. Of course, my hope is that God would eventually bring healing to your relationship, but in the meantime, you can honor them from a distance with your prayers.

But also give praise to God for who he created your parents to be and thank him for the gifts he has given you through them. At times, it may also be appropriate for your children to hear you confess your sin against your parents—especially if you sinned in front of your kids. It's good for our children to see us repenting of our failure to obey God's commands and turning to Christ for forgiveness and help.

The command to honor our parents comes with a promise—"that it might go well with you" (Eph. 6:3). While this promise doesn't guarantee us a life of wealth, health, or ease, it reminds us that God *does* intend spiritual good for those who obey his commands. By training our kids to honor their parents by honoring our own, our families are ready to receive His blessing.

May God empower you and your children to do his will, and may he bless your family for generations and generations to come!

# Children are Heritage

**Parallel Verses**

**New International Version**

Children are a heritage from the LORD, offspring a reward from him.

**New Living Translation**

Children are a gift from the LORD; they are a reward from him.

**English Standard Version**

Behold, children are a heritage from the LORD, the fruit of the womb a reward.

**New American Standard Bible**

Behold, children are a gift of the LORD, The fruit of the womb is a reward.

**King James Bible**

Lo, children *are* an heritage of the LORD: *and* the fruit of the womb *is his* reward.

**Holman Christian Standard Bible**

Sons are indeed a heritage from the LORD, children, a reward.

## International Standard Version

Children are a gift from the LORD; a productive womb, the LORD's reward.

## NET Bible

Yes, sons are a gift from the LORD, the fruit of the womb is a reward.

## New Heart English Bible

Behold, children are a heritage of the LORD. The fruit of the womb is his reward.

## Aramaic Bible in Plain English

For the inheritance of Lord Jehovah is children, the reward of the fruit of the womb.

## GOD'S WORD® Translation

Children are an inheritance from the LORD. They are a reward from him.

## JPS Tanakh 1917

Lo, children are a heritage of the LORD; The fruit of the womb is a reward.

## New American Standard 1977

Behold, children are a gift of the LORD;

The fruit of the womb is a reward.


## Jubilee Bible 2000

Behold, sons are a heritage of the LORD, and the fruit of the womb is to be desired.


## King James 2000 Bible

Lo, children are a heritage of the LORD: and the fruit of the womb is his reward.


## American King James Version

See, children are an heritage of the LORD: and the fruit of the womb is his reward.


## American Standard Version

Lo, children are a heritage of Jehovah; And the fruit of the womb is his reward.


## Douay-Rheims Bible

behold the inheritance of the Lord are children: the reward, the fruit of the womb.

## Darby Bible Translation

Lo, children are an inheritance from Jehovah, [and] the fruit of the womb a reward.

## English Revised Version

Lo, children are heritage of the LORD: and the fruit of the womb is his reward.

## Webster's Bible Translation

Lo, children are a heritage of the LORD: and the fruit of the womb is his reward.

## World English Bible

Behold, children are a heritage of Yahweh. The fruit of the womb is his reward.

## Young's Literal Translation

Lo, an inheritance of Jehovah are sons, A reward is the fruit of the womb.

## Commentary

# The Value of the Divine Blessing

*Psalm 127:3 Commentaries*

Let us always look to God's providence. In all the affairs and business of a family we must depend upon his blessing. For raising a family. If God be not acknowledged, wehave no reason to expect his blessing; and the best-laid plans fail, unless he crowns them with success.

For the safety of a family let us always look to God. Except the Lord keep the city, the watchmen, though they neither slumber nor sleep, wake but in vain; mischief may break out, which even early discoveries may not be able to prevent.

For enriching a family. Some are so eager upon the world, that they are continually full of care, which makes their comforts bitter and their lives a burden.

All this is to get money; but all in vain, except God prosper them: while those who love the Lord, using due diligence in their lawful callings, and casting all their care upon him, have needful success, without uneasiness or vexation. Our care must be to keep ourselves in the love of God; then we may be easy, whether we have little or much of this world. But we must use the proper means very diligently.

Children are God's gifts, a heritage, and a reward; and are to be accounted blessings, and not burdens: he who sends mouths, will send meat, if we trust in him. They are a great support and defense to a family. Children who are young, may be directed upright to the mark, God's glory, and the service of their generation; but when they are gone into the world, they are arrows out of the hand, it is too late to direct them then.

But these arrows in the hand too often prove arrows in the heart, a grief to godly parents. Yet, if trained according to God's word, they generally prove the best defense in declining years, remembering their obligations to their parents, and taking care of them in old age. All earthly comforts are uncertain, but the Lord will assuredly comfort and bless those who serve him; and those who seek the conversion of sinners, will find that their spiritual children are their joy and crown in the day of Jesus Christ.

## Unless the Lord Builds

It is vain for you to rise up early, To retire late, To eat the bread of painful labors; For He gives to His beloved even in his sleep. 3Behold, children are a gift of the LORD, The fruit of the womb is a reward. Like arrows in the hand of a warrior, So are the children of one's youth....

*New American Standard Bible*

## Cross References

### Genesis 1:28

God blessed them; and God said to them, "Be fruitful and multiply, and fill the earth, and subdue it; and rule over the fish of the sea and over the birds of the sky and over every living thing that moves on the earth."

### Genesis 25:21

Isaac prayed to the LORD on behalf of his wife, because she was barren; and the LORD answered him and Rebekah his wife conceived.

### Genesis 33:5

He lifted his eyes and saw the women and the children, and said, "Who are these with you?" So he said, "The children whom God has graciously given your servant."

### Genesis 48:4

and He said to me, 'Behold, I will make you fruitful and numerous, and I will make you a company of peoples, and will give this land to your descendants after you for an everlasting possession.'

### Deuteronomy 7:13

"He will love you and bless you and multiply you; He will also bless the fruit of your womb and the fruit of your ground, your grain and your new wine and your oil, the increase of your herd and the young of your flock, in the land which He swore to your forefathers to give you.

### Deuteronomy 28:4

"Blessed shall be the offspring of your body and the produce of your ground and the offspring of your beasts, the increase of your herd and the young of your flock.

### Joshua 24:3

'Then I took your father Abraham from beyond the River, and led him through all the land of Canaan, and multiplied his descendants and gave him Isaac.

### Joshua 24:4

'To Isaac I gave Jacob and Esau, and to Esau I gave Mount Seir to possess it; but Jacob and his sons went down to Egypt.

### Psalm 113:9

He makes the barren woman abide in the house As a joyful mother of children. Praise the LORD!

### Isaiah 13:18

And their bows will mow down the young men, They will not even have compassion on the fruit of the womb, Nor will their eye pity children.

### Treasury of Scripture

*See, children are an heritage of the LORD: and the fruit of the womb is his reward.***Children**

# Stepping Into Parenting

Arguing? Complaining? Nagging? Bargaining? Giving up? Bending rules? Begging? You need this book. In our most critical job, we often find ourselves in loops of negativity when it comes to parenting our intensely wonderful, but often challenging, children. Using the three stands of Howard Glasser's Nurtured Heart Approach®, Tammy (Small) Fisher tackles common parenting dilemmas with the lens focused on children's good choices, empowering parents to let go of ineffective habits of interaction and rediscover their own gifts and those of their children.

Transforming the Difficult Child brings to life a new way of shifting intense children to a solid life of success. The Nurtured Heart Approach puts a refreshing spin on both parenting and teaching and reveals new techniques and strategies that create thoroughly positive behaviors. This is the newly updated 2008 revision.

Transforming the Difficult Child brings to life a new way of shifting intense children to a solid life of success. The Nurtured Heart Approach puts a refreshing spin on both parenting and teaching and reveals new techniques and strategies that create thoroughly positive behaviors. This is the newly updated 2008 revision.

In *Raising Human Beings*, the internationally renowned child psychologist and *New York Times* bestselling author of *Lost at School* and *The Explosive Child* explains how to cultivate a better parent-child relationship while also nurturing empathy, honesty, resilience, and independence.

Parents have an important task: figure out who their child is--his or her skills, preferences, beliefs, values, personality traits, goals, and direction--get comfortable with it, and then help him or her pursue and live a life that is congruent with it. But parents also want to have influence. They want their kid to be independent, but not if he or she is going to make bad choices. They don't want to be harsh and rigid, but nor do they want a noncompliant, disrespectful kid. They want to avoid being too pushy and overbearing, but not if an unmotivated, apathetic kid is what they have to show for it. They

want to have.

In *Raising Human Beings*, the internationally renowned child psychologist and *New York Times* bestselling author of *Lost at School* and *The Explosive Child* explains how to cultivate a better parent-child relationship while also nurturing empathy, honesty, resilience, and independence.

Parents have an important task: figure out who their child is--his or her skills, preferences, beliefs, values, personality traits, goals, and direction--get comfortable with it, and then help him or her pursue and live a life that is congruent with it. But parents also want to have influence. They want their kid to be independent, but not if he or she is going to make bad choices. They don't want to be harsh and rigid, but nor do they want a noncompliant, disrespectful kid. They want to avoid being too pushy and overbearing, but not if an unmotivated, apathetic kid is what they have to show for it. They want to provide educators with highly practical, explicit guidance on implementing his evidence-based *Collaborative & Proactive Solutions* (CPS) model with behaviorally-challenging students. While the first two books described Dr. Greene's non-punitive, non-adversarial approach and described implementation on a macro level, *Lost & Found* provides more explicit.

Stepping into Stepfathering is a book about the ups and downs of Stepfathering. Written by a Stepfather, for Stepfathers, especially stepfathers-to-be or new Stepfathers, it contains a wealth of useful experience, advice, hints, tips and knowledge, all of which can help to ease the difficulties a new Stepfather may encounter. Well worth the money - a fine read!

# How to talk so children will listen

Dealing with drama

The things that are really important are not the things you see; some people would believe, the more things they provide for their children is how determine their love for their children. The love you provide for your children by spending more time and not spending more money. What have you gained from spending more money and not enough time. Some people think if I put my child in sports are activities that is spending time with them. My mother never attended any sports activities. She spent time making quilts and homemade dishes like teacakes, egg pies and jelly rolls , fried prune pies. stitching socks and sowing on buttons. Helping with homework. My mother was a domestic engineer, the antiquated words would be staying home mom.

It was not a choice to go to church. When my mother said "lets go," we were already walking toward the door.

In *Parenting from the Inside Out*, child psychiatrist Daniel J. Siegel, M.D., and early childhood expert Mary Hartzell, M.Ed., explore the extent to which our childhood experiences shape the way we parent. Drawing on stunning new findings in neurobiology and attachment research, they explain how interpersonal relationships directly impact the development of the brain, and offer parents a step-by-step approach to forming a deeper understanding of their own life stories, which will help them raise compassionate and resilient children.

Have you ever stepped back to watch what really goes on when your children play? As psychologist Lawrence J. Cohen points out, play is children's way of exploring the world, communicating deep feelings, getting close to those they care about, working through stressful situations, and simply blowing off steam. That's why "playful parenting" is so important and so successful in building strong, close bonds between parents and children. Through play we join our kids in *their* world–and help them to live.

# POEM WRITTEN BY
## Dr. Shirley Durham

Parenting Isn't Easy You May Say

I get up every morning wondering

what my children will have today.

I lay down at night

Asking  God to make everything alright.

He reminds me,

I am with you in the still of the Night.

You are the Parent that God allow you to be.

Instructing your children to be in the Image of God

Is what He has intended them to be.